WESSEX LANDSCAPES
A POET'S JOURNEY

Wessex Landscapes

A Poet's Journey

Amanda K Hampson

Illustrated by
Sheila Haley

THE HOBNOB PRESS

First published in the United Kingdom in 2025

by The Hobnob Press,
8 Lock Warehouse, Severn Road, Gloucester GL1 2GA
www.hobnobpress.co.uk

© Amanda K Hampson and Sheila Haley 2025

The Author and Illustrator hereby assert their moral rights to be identified as the Authors of the Work.

All rights reserved. No part of this publication may be reproduced, stored in a retrieval system, or transmitted in any form or by any means, electronic, mechanical, photocopying, recording or otherwise, without the prior permission of the publisher and copyright holder.

British Library Cataloguing in Publication Data
A catalogue record for this book is available from the British Library

ISBN 978-1-914407-82-6 (paperback)
ISBN 978-1-914407-83-3 (hardback)

Typeset in Adobe Garamond Pro 12/14 pt.
Typesetting and origination by John Chandler

*'Better far than this to stray about
Voluptuously through fields and rural walks
And ask no record of the hours given up'*

William Wordsworth
The Prelude

Contents

Introductory Note

Fugitives by Simon Armitage

The Quantock Hills	1
Blue Anchor Bay	3
Lines from Nether Stowey	4
The Seven Sisters	7
Dead Woman's Ditch	8
At Kilve	10
Horse Chestnut	11
Cantuctun	12
Cranborne Chase and the North Wessex Downs	13
The King's Chase	16
Chalk Stream	17
Dark Skies	18
The Road to Everleigh - Four Haiku	19
The Goldfinch	21
Lombardy Poplars	22
Wessex Chalk	23
Dorset and the Blackdown Hills	25
Colmer's Hill	27
Pilsdon Pen	29
Kingcombe Meadows	30
At Arne	31
Far from the Madding Crowd	32
The Blackdown Hills	34
What, No Towns?	35

The Mendip Hills and the Somerset Levels	37
Dry-stone Wall	39
Wind Turbine	40
Peregrine	41
Sky-dancer I	43
Sky-dancer II	44
Willow	45
Teasel	47
Some Wessex Poets	49
Samuel Taylor Coleridge	49
William Wordsworth	49
Edward Thomas	55
Anne Ridler	57
William Lisle Bowles	58
Alfred Williams	61
Thomas Hardy	62
Charlotte Smith	66
William Barnes	67
Henry Alford	70
About the Author	73
The Artist	73
Other Titles by the Author	74

Introductory Note

Wessex Landscapes, A Poet's Journey is my third collection of poetry inspired by the natural world. There are 46 National Landscapes in the UK (formerly known as Areas of Outstanding Natural Beauty), and simply put, they are areas of distinctive character and natural beauty that are protected in the national interest.

On my journey in poetry I take the reader through six National Landscapes in Wessex, starting with the Quantock Hills, travelling through Cranborne Chase and the North Wessex Downs, Dorset and the Blackdown Hills, and ending with the Mendip Hills; I also strayed into the Somerset Levels, which are low-lying between the Quantocks and the Mendips. Along the way I found some rich connections with celebrated poets, and in addition to my own poems, I have delved into the lives of well-known poets who have also been inspired by these landscapes.

I am delighted to be able to preface my work with the poem *Fugitives*, from the current Poet Laureate, Simon Armitage. Simon was commissioned in 2019 by the (then) National Association for Areas of Outstanding Natural Beauty, to write a poem to celebrate the 70th anniversary of the National Parks and Access to the Countryside Act. His poem appears on the following pages, together with a short biography.

My thanks go to Sheila Haley for her beautiful illustrations accompanying my poems; to my husband Keith for all his technical support and valuable comments; and to John Chandler of Hobnob Press, for bringing to publication what I hope is an attractive and enjoyable book of poetry.

Amanda K Hampson
December 2024

Fugitives by Simon Armitage

*Then we woke and were hurtling headlong
for wealds and wolds,
blood coursing, the Dee and the Nidd in full spate
through the spinning waterwheels in the wrists
and over the heart's weir,
the nightingale hip-hopping ten to the dozen
under the morning's fringe.*

*It was no easy leap, to exit the engine house of the head
and vault the electric fence
of commonplace things,
to open the door of the century's driverless hearse,
roll from the long cortège
then dust down and follow
the twisting ribbon of polecats wriggling free from extinction
or slipstream the red kite's triumphant flypast out of oblivion
or trail the catnip of spraint and scat tingeing
the morning breeze.*

*On we journeyed at full tilt
through traffic-light orchards,
the brain's compass dialling for fell, moor,
escarpment and shore, the skull's sextant
plotting for free states coloured green on the map,
using hedgerows as handrails,
barrows and crags as trig points and cats' eyes.*

*We stuck to the switchbacks and scenic routes,
steered by the earth's contours and natural lines of desire,
feet firm on solid footings of bedrock and soil
fracked only by moles.
We skimmed across mudflat and saltmarsh,
clambered to stony pulpits on high hills*

inhaling gallons of pure sky
into the moors of our lungs,
bartered bitcoins of glittering shingle and shale.

Then arrived in safe havens, entered the zones,
stood in the grandstands of bluffs and ghylls, spectators
to flying ponies grazing wild grass to carpeted lawns,
oaks flaunting turtle doves on their ring-fingers,
ospreys fishing the lakes from invisible pulleys and hoists,
the falcon back on its see-through pivot, lured from its gyre.

Here was nature as future,
the satellite dishes of blue convolvulus
tuned to the cosmos, tracking the chatter of stars,
the micro-gadgets of complex insects
working the fields, heaths tractored by beetles,
rainbowed hay meadows tipsy with mist and light,
golden gravel hoarded in eskers and streams.

And we vowed not to slumber again
but claimed sanctuary
under the kittiwake's siren
and corncrake's alarm,
in realms patrolled by sleepwalking becks and creeks
where beauty employs its own border police.

And witnessed ancient trees
affirming their citizenship of the land,
and hunkered and swore oaths, made laws
in hidden parliaments of bays and coves,
then gathered on commons and capes
waving passports of open palms, medalled by dog rose and teasel
and raising the flag of air.

Copyright © Simon Armitage

I love this poem from Simon Armitage; what a perfect opener for my journey through some National Landscapes. Every line is richly evocative of a break for freedom, an escape from everyday life, and a carefree roaming of the English countryside.

I particularly love these lines:
'It was no easy leap, to exit the engine house of the head
and vault the electric fence
of commonplace things,'

'…the brain's compass dialling for fell, moor,
escarpment and shore, the skull's sextant
plotting for free states coloured green on the map,'

A wonderful use of metaphor – such a powerful tool in poetry.
Amanda K Hampson

Simon Armitage was born in West Yorkshire and is Professor of Poetry at the University of Leeds. A recipient of numerous prizes and awards, he has written over twenty collections of poetry, writes extensively for television and radio, and is the author of two novels and three bestselling non-fiction books. His theatre works include The Last Days of Troy, performed at the Shakespeare's Globe in 2014. From 2015 to 2019, he served as Professor of Poetry at the University of Oxford, and in 2018, he was awarded the Queen's Gold Medal for Poetry. Simon Armitage is Poet Laureate.

The Quantock Hills

A Home to the Romantic Poets

The Quantock Hills were England's first Area of Outstanding Natural Beauty (now a National Landscape), designated in 1956. The Hills, which lie west of Bridgwater in Somerset, predominantly consist of heathland, oak woodlands, ancient parklands and agricultural areas. The Hills were first named in Saxon charters around AD 880 as *Cantuctun,* and two centuries later in the Domesday Book as *Cantoctona* and *Cantetone* – with *Cantuc* being Celtic for a rim or circle, and *ton* or *tun* Old English for a settlement.

This etymological background seemed to me to be a rich vein for poetic composition. In my poem entitled *Cantuctun,* in the style of a villanelle, I have tried to link the notion of a circle of hills with a musical round, working with the derivatives of the Latin *cantare* (to sing). The villanelle is the perfect poetic form for such an evocation – it circles round and round, suggesting powerful recurrences of mood and emotion. The form consists of repeated lines, representing economy of effort for the poet!

The Quantocks are notable for their connection to some celebrated poets; Samuel Taylor Coleridge lived in Nether Stowey in the late 18th Century, and in his memory the Coleridge Way was set up as a long-distance trail, starting in Nether Stowey and finishing in Porlock. William Wordsworth and his sister Dorothy lived near to Coleridge at the same time, and through their friendship, Wordsworth and Coleridge created the so-called *Lyrical Ballads,* which heralded the start of the English Romantic Movement in poetry in England – more of this in the chapter entitled **Some Wessex Poets**. *Lines from Nether Stowey,* is written through the eyes of Coleridge, and contains some short excerpts from both Coleridge and Wordsworth.

On a brief but rewarding visit to the Quantocks one February, we walked from Nether Stowey to the beach at Kilve, and the changing colours and increasing wind speed as we approached the coast, sparked some thoughts for the short poem *At Kilve*. On arriving at the beach, from where the construction work at Hinkley Point was clearly visible, we were surprised to see what appeared to be an oil platform out at sea, lit up in the pale Winter sunshine; two very contrasting sources of energy.

Another coastal spot, *Blue Anchor Bay*, lent itself to a pacy rhyming poem of the same name. Here the coloured alabaster found in the cliffs gave rise to the name 'Watchet Blue'. The seaside village takes its name from a seventeenth century inn; the bay and the inn were the subjects of a watercolour painting by JMW Turner in 1818.

Climbing up to one of the high points on the Quantocks known as Cothelstone Hill, we were met with some friendly-looking ponies, which were sheltering under the landmark clump of beech trees known as *The Seven Sisters*; the vista seemed to lend itself to a rhyming poem.

In the centre of the Quantocks landscape we find *Dead Woman's Ditch* – a linear earthwork consisting of a bank and a ditch about one kilometre long. Most of the available images of this ancient monument are rather gloomy, reflecting the somewhat sinister tales of murder associated with it, although it is said that the structure received its name prior to any criminal wrongdoings.

On a return trip to the Quantocks one May, I couldn't help but be inspired to write about the *Horse Chestnut* trees laden with white flowers – not unique to the area, but worthy of a poem.

Blue Anchor Bay

Oh cliffs of alabaster blue
that brighten the mudstone hue!
At Old Cleeve's Blue Anchor Bay,
with its sparkling sands and spray,
a scene for J W Turner,
who painted the glittering vista,
that drew the Rev Richard Warner,
among other West Country ramblers,
to stay at the Blue Anchor Inn,
where James Savage had also been,
and declared the view as grand,
across the lawn to the strand,
where Watchet Blue can be reached,
as long as the sea hasn't breached,
the inlet at Warren Bay,
it's only a short walk away.
But why was Blue Anchor Bay so named?
The clay stuck to a ship's anchor it's claimed.
Oh cliffs of alabaster blue
that lift the mudstone hue!

Lines from Nether Stowey

Coleridge

Through our garden gate I wander,
to the lime-tree bower
that is my writing place in Nether Stowey.
Through clumsy accident I am obliged
to sit beneath its nodding branches
while my friends walk the hills,
our beloved hills,
'Well, they are gone, and here I must remain,
This lime-tree bower my prison!'

So I shall write,
and these are my imaginings:

'On springy heath, along the hill-top edge,
Wander in gladness… To that still roaring dell…
o'erwooded, narrow deep,
And only speckled by the mid-day sun…
…Pale beneath the blaze
Hung the transparent foliage; and I watched
Some broad and sunny leaf, and loved to see
The shadow of the leaf and the stem above
Dappling its sunshine!…'

Wordsworth

I walk and talk every day with my sister Dorothy
and my friend Coleridge;
though today, through injury, Samuel remains
in Nether Stowey!

Wandering the hills is at the heart of our relationship;
my sister spoke thus:
*'We lay sidelong upon the turf,
And gazed on the landscape
till it melted into more than natural loveliness.'*

Dorothy gave me eyes, she gave me ears!
*'Upon smooth Quantock's airy ridge we roved, unchecked, or loitered
'mid her sylvan combes.'*

And from *The Prelude*:
*'Better far than this to stray about
Voluptuously through fields and rural walks
And ask no record of the hours given up...'*

And I was inspired thus:
The Thorn
*'High on a mountain's highest ridge,
Where oft the stormy winter gale
Cuts like a scythe, while through the clouds
It sweeps from vale to vale;
Not five yards from the mountain path,
This thorn you on your left espy;
And to the left, three yards beyond,
You see a little muddy pond
Of water – never dry,
Though but of compass small, and bare
To thirsty suns and parching air.'*

Coleridge and I call ourselves the Nature Poets!
We rail against the highly-sculpted poetry
that has gone before,
believing that our writing should be borne of emotion,

rather than reason and intellect.
We re-imagine the way poetry should sound,
focusing on individual experience;
isolation and melancholy are common themes!
We celebrate nature and the common man -
and so our *Lyrical Ballads* were conceived,
and the Romantic Movement in England was born!

*'Poetry is the spontaneous overflow of powerful feelings:
it takes its origin in emotion recollected in tranquility.'*

The Seven Sisters

Atop the heath of Cothelstone Hill
stand some beech trees tall and still.
The crowning glory of a lovely vista,
known on the Quantocks as the Seven Sisters.
But only a few trees now remain,
perhaps the lie of the land helps to explain;
they were planted on a circular mound
with nothing much else around,
and since beech trees have shallow roots,
this would no doubt contribute
to the fall of a circular planting,
the demise of a landmark tree ring.
It was meant to be ornamental,
a sort of arboreal pinnacle,
looking down on a panoramic view.
And until a storm blows through,
the clump of trees remains, tall and still
atop the heath of Cothelstone Hill.

Dead Woman's Ditch

Dead Woman's Ditch
begins at Lady's Fountain,
a name that belies
a gruesome history
of this ancient earthwork.

Where whortleberries grow
an ill-wind blows.

She was the Walford wife,
murdered at Dead Woman's Ditch
by her husband in seventeen-eighty-nine.
And her wandering ghost
seeks justice still.

Whortleberry blue
hides a macabre view.

She drifts after dusk
among gnarled and stunted oaks
that twist away to a lightless sky,
from ancient mossy seats
on leaf-littered banks.

Whortleberry mounds
where evil is found.

These contorted trees,
with their cankered knots and ugly notches,
shroud this sinister tale
that ended with Walford hanged,
and swinging in a gibbet for a year.

*Whortleberry leaves turn red
with the blood of the dead.*

And two hundred years after Walford's wife,
the remains of another were discovered
near this Iron Age ditch,
where the trees lean in
and whisper of the dead.

*Where whortleberries grow
an ill-wind blows.*

At Kilve

As we walk towards the sea
the flattening land drains itself of colour,
the sky lowers herself
into billowing greys,
and the blackthorns strain towards us
on the westerly wind.
Are they greeting us or warning us?
Through soft mists that smudge the horizon,
cranes puncture the sky at Hinkley,
and the shiny legs of an oil platform
are lit up
in a blaze of sunshine.

Horse Chestnut

The greenest of trees,
waving from the front row
of its roadside theatre.
Fresh and lush,
its palmate leaves emerge in Spring,
hanging like a drooping hand,
on pendulous boughs
candled at their tips
with the palest flowers;
panicles like small frosted Christmas trees.
And then the bees come. And come.

How is it
that a flower so delicate in Spring
has a fruit glossy and hard in Autumn?
A conker shining brown
through a split in its spiky case,
ready to fall.
As the days shorten,
those leaves droop once again,
this time shrivelled with Autumn senescence,
and a moth that mines their veins.

Cantuctun

The Latin for 'sing' is cantare
A choral work is a cantata
A musical round is a circle

The Celtic for circle is cantuc
A Simple melody is a cantillena
The Latin for 'sing' is cantare

A settlement is a 'ton' or 'tun'
Music in a singing style is cantabile
A musical round is a circle

A circle of hills round a settlement is a cantuctun
To chant in musical tones is to cantillate
The Latin for sing is cantare

The Domesday book cites Quantocks as Cantetone
Another word for a hymn is a canticle
A musical round is a circle

We have come full circle
Cantuctun and Cantetone are the Quantocks
The Latin for 'sing' is cantare
A musical round is a circle

Cranborne Chase and the North Wessex Downs

Downs, combes, knolls and ridges

The National Landscape of Cranborne Chase covers 380 square miles of countryside, overlapping the boundaries of Wiltshire, Dorset, Hampshire and Somerset. It offers a rich and diverse natural landscape, with rare chalk grasslands, scientifically important ancient woodlands, and chalk escarpments. The downland hillsides and chalk river valleys have a distinct and recognizable character.

Sitting on the extensive belt of chalkland which stretches across southern England, the Chase is divided into two areas by the fertile wooded Vale of Wardour. To the south are smooth rounded downs, steeply cut combes and dry valleys, typical of a chalk landscape. To the north, the topography is more varied and broken, with shapely knolls and whaleback ridges. Both areas are fringed on the west by an impressive scarp, cresting above the adjoining clay vales.

Cranborne Chase is of great ecological importance. Its protected sites include scattered deciduous woodland, some of which supports remnants of the ancient Cranborne Chase hunting forest and the former Royal Forests of Selwood and Gillingham. 'This was the hunting ground of kings' (*The King's Chase*).

Since 2019 the Chase has been an International Dark Sky Reserve (IDSR). As such, it engages communities to continually improve its dark skies by limiting artificial light pollution, while encouraging enjoyment through improved access. At the time of its designation, Cranborne Chase became the 14th IDSR in the world, and was the only National Landscape to be designated as such in its entirety. The Reserve features in the poem *Dark Skies*, which poses some unfathomable questions about the measureless universe.

From remote, rolling downland to picture postcard villages, the walking country of the North Wessex Downs National Landscape straddles Wiltshire, Berkshire, Hampshire and Oxfordshire. The chalk landscape here has formed the wide-open downland, dramatic scarp slopes, majestic ancient woodland and sheltered river valleys.

The two landscapes featured in this chapter are notable for their chalk streams; in fact a large proportion of chalk streams globally are in southern England. Important for the wildlife and ecology they support, these rivers rise from springs in areas with chalk bedrock, and the waters are usually crystal clear. This beauty I hope is captured in the poem *Chalk Stream*.

The importance of downland habitat, ancient woodland and chalk streams is reflected in major projects undertaken by the National Landscapes Association, including the 'Big Chalk' project - an ambitious programme that aims to restore a mosaic of habitats on a huge scale across the calcareous (chalk and limestone) landscapes of southern England. Due to their underlying geology and history, these areas are particularly species rich, and provide an exceptional opportunity for wildlife to thrive and adapt to climate change. The Big Chalk project inspired my poem entitled *Wessex Chalk*. Here and there in my poems in this book, you will note references to the climate emergency.

There is some fun to be had with haiku – a three-line Japanese poem that can be read in one breath, and conveys a sense of sudden enlightenment and illumination. Haiku often focuses on images from nature and emphasizes simplicity, intensity and directness of expression. My four haiku here pick up on themes from the Pewsey Vale in *The Road to Everleigh*. Also in the Pewsey Vale, I have seen the occasional line of *Lombardy poplars*, which can look breathtaking in winter with the skeletal branches pinned against a crimson sky in the twilight.

Finally, as James Rebanks describes in his book *English Pastoral*, farmland can quickly become choked with thistles and ragwort. But the goldfinch's liking for thistle seeds conjures up the vibrant image of these birds swaying on top of the lovely thistle purple flowers, as pictured in the artwork accompanying *The Goldfinch* in this chapter.

The King's Chase

Going west,
there's a stretch of the A303,
near Fontmell Bishop,
where the hawthorn hedges fall away,
and the gaze of our passengers
drifts left…
to where one chalk down folds into another,
where a patchwork of yellow and green
invades the downland in Spring,
where tartan fields are laid out like
handkerchiefs in Autumn,
and where steeply cut combes
cleave smooth rounded hills.
Forested centuries ago,
this was the hunting ground of kings.
And the oak and the ash and the bonny ivy tree
have returned
where the land has been exhausted by crops.

Chalk Stream

Gin-clear, your waters course through the chalk,
swelling your riffles and swirling deeps.
You smooth-ripple over crowfoot,
whirling through watercress,
eddying round fallen branches,
tinkling over rocks.
Constant motion, constant sound.

And where your waters slow,
you drop gravel to gleaming flinted beds,
where fish flick, and happily spawn.
Dipper bobs on a wet-brown boulder,
swollen white breast flashing a warning.
Kingfisher cuts a sharp line
through trailing willows.
A heron lifts heavily from the bank
and barrels majestically
down your valley,
the one you created long ago.
Timeless motion, timeless sound.

Dark Skies

Looking up, at the out there,
a blanket of midnight blue
is pinned to the edge of the universe
by infinite twinklings.
Untainted by light bleeding upwards
from Planet Earth
Where does it begin?
Where does it end?

The Milky Way
is like a glittering mare's tail
of numberless stars
unfathomable light years away –
insignificant in a swirling galaxy
in the measureless universe!
Where does it begin?
Where does it end?

And we wonder if other life
is out there.
But who's to say what life is?
We can only conceive of living things
within our own frame of thinking
and our own discoveries.
Where does it all begin?
Where does it end?

The Road to Everleigh – Four Haiku

Up on the hill the pigs are free-ranging
little Nissen huts for when it's raining.
And when we slay them we betray them

One day on that road after dark
we saw the barn was licked with flames.
Weeks later, sunbeams danced on a shiny new one

We always thought it would be exciting to see tanks on
the Trenchard lines
but then one day we saw them thundering down the gravel.
It was quite creepy

Driving up that hill, dropping the gears, past the white
horse
the village was gradually swallowed by mantling trees.
Our dwelling, hidden in the Vale

The Goldfinch

Even the stony pastureland
was choked by thistles;
a waist-high sea of parched burr prickles,
hostile to all
save for a goldfinch,
swaying from its lookout post on purple flowers,
pecking hungrily at the thistle seeds.

And so we took our scythes, whetstone-sharpened,
in the heat and dust
of the waning Summer,
slashing at thistles, ragwort too.
The snaith straining with each swing,
the flashing blade messed with thistle sap.
Swifts and swallows
cleaved the air all about us,
hoping for clouds of insects.
And scythe. And scythe. And scythe.

And so the bird's perch was imperilled,
and the goldfinch vanished
in a splendour of wing-gold.
And scythe. And scythe. And scythe.

Lombardy Poplars

Lonely the colonnade stands,
at the edge of the field in winter,
leafless, shadeless, soundless.
Bare skeletons are feathered
against the pinking clouds scudding by,
like the delicate tracery of a fossil fern.
No companion for the clodded earth below,
barren and spiked with crop remains,
Winter-sodden in the low-lying Vale.

But gently a whispering wind returns,
caressing emergent silvered leaves,
as they flutter this way and that.
And light and shade strengthen again,
the bowery canopy sheltering the field below.
Small birds flit and chatter high up,
ornaments on outstretched branches.
And the poplars from Lombardy
are lonely no more.

Wessex Chalk

In an arc from Wessex to mid-England
sweeps a rich calcareous downland,
where swathes of grassland flourish
on chalk from the cretaceous.
Once vigorous scrub and woodland,
farming has changed these lowlands,
and centuries have seen habitat loss,
sacrificed to provide food for us.
Now global warming presents a challenge too,
and we risk plant species becoming rather few.

So,

let us help these fragile populations
in a bid for climate change mitigation,
and start with restoration
to enable transformation
and encourage adaptation
for new habitat creation.

Dorset and the Blackdown Hills

Land of Hardy and Hills

Covering some 44 percent of Dorset, the National Landscape stretches along one of Britain's finest coastlines, and reaching inland, takes in countryside that still evokes the settings of Thomas Hardy's novels and poetry. The rural landscape varies from the ridges and valleys of central Dorset, through chalk ridges and limestone plateau to the sandy heaths and flats of Poole Harbour. In 2001, the Jurassic Coast became England's first natural World Heritage site, being recognized as a place of outstanding universal value, to be protected, conserved and passed intact to future generations. It provided me with great riches for the poetry in my second book – *The Jurassic Coast: A Poet's Journey*.

Here we move to the inland National Landscape for inspiration. *Pilsdon Pen* is a notable high spot in the Marshwood Vale, from where other landmarks, Colmer's Hill and Golden Cap, are clearly visible. The sea glitters in the distance, making it a special place to visit. I have included a quote from Dorothy Wordsworth at the start of the poem, which draws a parallel between the Dorset hills and the Wordsworth's 'native wilds' (the Lake District). We hear more about the Wordsworths in the chapter on the Quantocks, and indeed in the second half of this book, on Wessex poets.

Two of the inspirations in this chapter lend themselves to the poetic form known as the pantoum; it is the perfect form for the evocation of a past time. It allows the reader to relax, since all the lines make a second appearance – what was missed the first time, can be picked up on the second. It is also less demanding for the poet, as only half the number of original lines is needed, compared with other poetic forms! Thus, the history of *Colmer's Hill* is told, and *Far from the Madding Crowd* talks of Egdon Heath, a fictitious area of Hardy's Wessex . The latter is the second of my poems with this title, the first appearing in the aforementioned book of my journey along the Jurassic Coast. The inspiration for this second poem came from a sketch of Black Heath Corner in Dorset – Thomas Hardy's first attempt at sketching from nature.

I mentioned above the sandy heaths and flats of Poole Harbour; close by is the wonderful RSPB nature reserve at Arne, where I spotted my first avocet. *At Arne* hopefully captures the beauty of this heathland nature reserve. By contrast, the lovely *Kingcombe Meadows* Wildlife Trust nature reserve, still worked as an old-fashioned farm, is tucked away in delightful countryside off the road between Crewkerne and Dorchester.

The Blackdown Hills present perhaps a lesser known National Landscape, but notable for their unique features nonetheless. The Blackdown Hills lie on the border of Devon and Somerset, and are best known for the dramatic, steep wooded scarp face in the north. To the south the land dips away gently as a plateau, deeply dissected by valleys, in which villages and hamlets nestle, surrounded by ancient and intricate patterns of small enclosed fields and a maze of winding high-hedged lanes. What makes this area special is the unspoilt rural character of the 'ordinary' landscape. Interestingly, there are no towns within the Blackdown Hills National Landscape, which remains sparsely populated; hence the poem entitled *What, no towns?* The isolated villages and farmsteads retain a quiet rustic charm, and using local materials – chertstone, cob and thatch – many of the buildings are of architectural interest and display a mix of styles. These and the narrow, ribboning lanes feature in the poem entitled simply *The Blackdown Hills*.

Colmer's Hill

This perfect conical landmark
cloaked with orangey bracken stands in Autumn,
carpeted with a wash of bluebells in Spring,
holds court over the land of Symondsbury.

Cloaked with orangey bracken stands in Autumn,
and so named after the Rev John Colmer,
it holds court over the land of Symondsbury,
owned by the Colfax family for over 100 years.

So named after the Rev John Colmer.
'Take a bucket, and fill it with soil,' said Major Colfax.
It's been in the Colfax family for over 100 years.
'And take the bucket to the top of the hill.'

'Take a bucket, and fill it with soil,' said Major Colfax.
His woodmen planted Caledonian pines in World War I.
'And take the bucket to the top of the hill.'
A Monterey pine was added in 2006.

His woodmen planted Caledonian pines in World War I.
Nine pines in all.
A Monterey pine was added in 2006.
And a trig point stands on the pinnacle.

Nine pines in all.
A grassy path winds up through the bracken.
A trig point stands on the pinnacle,
looking down over Marshwood Vale.

A grassy path winds up through the bracken.
This perfect conical landmark,

looking down over Marshwood Vale,
carpeted with a wash of bluebells in Spring.

Pilsdon Pen

'We have hills which, seen from a distance almost take the character of mountains, some cultivated nearly to their summits, others in their wild state covered with furze and broom. These delight me the most as they remind me of our native wilds.'
(Dorothy Wordsworth, 1797)

We used to drive up to the car park, gravel crunching,
  Mum and Dad stayed in the car, a picnic munching.
You and I would walk up the hill to Pilsdon Pen,
'twas the only way to see both land and sea, then.
But sometime later, the parish of Marshwood Vale,
don't get me wrong this is a happy tale,
they cut down the brambled hedge
that obscured the view from the car park's edge.
So now when we drive up to the car park, gravel crunching,
we all stay in the car, a picnic munching.
With a breathtaking view of land and sea,
we can all relax with a cup of tea.

Kingcombe Meadows

Kingcombe Meadows
where the kingcup grows,
glowing gold in ponds and brooks,
and along the meandering River Hooke.

Cowslip and harebell carpet slopes of chalk,
iridescent dragonflies hum the boardwalk.
Orchids abound, varieties at least three,
cool dark woodland consumes the valley.

Lowland moor-grass all purple and tussocky,
sneezewort and scabious where it's slightly boggy.
Rare newts inhabit scattered ponds,
ferns are everywhere curling their fronds.

Yellowhammer and linnet fly up from hedgerows,
clouds of butterflies dance in hay meadows.
A hidden landscape of timeless charm,
still worked as an old-fashioned farm.

Kingcombe Meadows
where the kingcup grows,
glowing gold in ponds and brooks,
and along the meandering River Hooke.

At Arne

There's a viewpoint at Arne
that takes in the rich beauty of heathland;
the stonechat swaying atop golden gorse,
dense clumps of purple heather,
stands of bracken with rusting fronds,
and leggy pines and silver birch
punctuating the undergrowth.
As the sky pinks at dusk,
and darkness falls over the heath,
waders gather on the feeding grounds,
curlews haunting the Autumn skies
with a bubbling, evocative call.

It was here that I saw my first avocet,
wading in the distant shimmering shallows,
sweeping its upcurved beak from side to side
in search of food on the mudflats.
Recurvirostra avosetta was lost to us
two hundred years ago, but was tempted back
across the big skies of East Anglia,
when the vast beaches
were flooded as a defence
in World War II.
Is it any wonder
that this striking bird with pied plumage
symbolises bird conservation in Britain?

Far from the Madding Crowd

We shaped the land, and it shaped us.
My Egdon Heath was a furzy, briery wilderness
peopled by men of the land,
from sunrise to sunset we were coppicing and hedge-laying.

My Egdon Heath was a furzy, briery wilderness.
And you, you became inwoven with the heath,
from sunrise to sunset we were coppicing and hedge-laying.
You could speak the tongue of the trees
and fruits and flowers.

And you, you became inwoven with the heath,
until the Dorset heathland became fields.
You could speak the tongue of the trees
and fruits and flowers,
and now we are so used to seeing fields.

The Dorset heathland became fields,
all crops and livestock.
And now we are so used to seeing fields,
we think the fields were there first.

All crops and livestock.
But now the heath is being restored.
The fields have been here so long we think they came first.
On a rale south from the cottage, there is my Egdon Heath

But now the heath is being restored.
We shaped the land, and it shaped us.
On a rale south from the cottage, there is my Egdon Heath,
peopled by men of the land.

The Blackdown Hills

I
Occasionally there are tunnels
of wet-brown beeches
clasping overhead;
boles bulging from root-hollows
clinging to shallow ditches.
Here the unwholesome dankness
nourishes moss-hung boughs
and the glossy tongue fern,
on lanes ribboning their way
up to the ridge.

II
There were rustic farmsteads of cob and thatch
nestled among scarp woodlands of hazel and ash.
Hillside livestock wandered slowly in the distance,
constant grazing, it seems a strange existence.
The plateau is scoured by windswept spaces,
its slopes sunken into valleys in several places.
Stinking iris and orchid fill meadow and mire
on the gently dipping slopes in Somersetshire.
The Culm twists and loops as its name suggests,
down to the River Exe further southwest.
No towns or cities punctuate these hills,
sparsely populated they have a wildness still.

What, No Towns?

What, no towns
 among the hills of Blackdown?
It's more rustic domiciles
and farming lifestyles;
in thorps peopled sparsely
it's mostly dairy.

Farmsteads of cherstone, cob and thatch,
architectural style that's hard to match.
In a maze of high-hedged lanes
crossing valleys cleaving windswept plains,
lie the hamlets of Yarcombe and Sheldon,
Whitestaunton and Churchstanton.

What, no towns
among the hills of Blackdown?
What does it matter,
there are jewels in the crown,
from dramatic scarp in the north
to the great iron age Hembury Fort.

The Mendip Hills and the Somerset Levels

Dry-stone Walls and Rich Wetlands

Stretching eastward from the Bristol Channel, The Mendips are a range of limestone hills forming an imposing ridge, rising like a rampart above the Somerset Levels. This landscape is the most southerly example of carboniferous limestone country, and geological action has produced spectacular underground formations, most notably Cheddar Gorge and Wookey Hole.

Dry-stone walls, unusual in southern England, are an important feature of this landscape, and help to create its distinctive character. Dividing pastureland into fields, the walls are constructed from local limestone, and are of botanical significance as they support some nationally scarce species. The ancient and gentle skill of dry-stone walling was inspiration for the poem entitled simply, *Dry-stone Wall*.

In the Second World War, a bombing decoy was constructed at Beacon Batch on Black Down, the highest spot on the Mendips; more recently, the mast of the Mendip transmitting station, micro-hydroelectric turbines and a wind turbine have been installed. Plans for wind turbines on the Mendips have been proposed and opposed at various times this century, and putting to one side views on the acceptability of these structures, to my mind they do have a sculptural appeal (*Wind Turbine*).

Of the many bird species found in the Mendips, the peregrine falcon, which has gradually recolonised the area since the 1980s, is particularly significant. It breeds on sea and inland cliffs, and on the faces of active and disused quarries. This majestic bird is renowned for its hunting speed, reaching over 200 mph, and has distinctive egg-yolk yellow talons and beak (*Peregrine*).

The Somerset Levels straddle the gap between The Mendips and The Quantocks, and my attention was taken by the richness of wildlife found in the distinctive wetlands of the Levels. In particular, the starling murmurations to be seen over the reedbeds are some of the most breathtaking in the country, and inspired two versions of one poem (*Skydancer I and II*). During the Winter months, large numbers of starlings visit Britain for the relative warmth of our island climate. As dusk arrives each day, the starlings set off for their communal roost in one of the most amazing natural spectacles of all. Flocks arrive from all directions, and as the numbers reach the tens and hundreds of thousands, the 'murmurations' (the name for a flying flock of starlings) take on incredible shapes in the sky, contracting and expanding and taking on a life of their own; swirling back and forth in ever more complex and beautiful patterns.

Willow has been cut and used on the Somerset Levels since mankind moved in to the area. Basket making from willow was a thriving industry here until the 1950s, but has severely declined since then; the Somerset Levels is now the only area in the UK where basket willow is still grown commercially. White willow trees are commonly seen along riverbanks, around lakes and in wet woodlands, and it is this habitat that is the subject of *Willow*.

Unusually perhaps, teasels have also been grown commercially on the Somerset Levels. Again, this industry has largely died out, although teasel heads are still sometimes used to give a finish to worsteds and snooker-table cloth. Previously, they were much more widely used in the processing of wool for the textile industry – specifically to raise the nap on woollen cloths. We tend to be familiar with the dried seed head of the teasel, often appearing in dried flower displays, but the influorescence in Summer is astonishingly beautiful, with rings of tiny purple flowers appearing, framed by curving bracts of vivid green (*Teasel*).

Dry-stone Wall

In places,
the snaking wall was slumped and bowed
into a saddle of fallen stones.
A dereliction exploited by the things we call weeds.

And so we set about re-building.
Shuffling and manoeuvring the larger stones,
the roughness rasping at our over-sized gloves.
A scraping like the pleasing sound
of an old bread-oven door sliding open.
Reading the stone,
feeling the stone,
settling the stones in place
between the taught string guides.
Pinging.
And tap, tap, tap with the hammer,
the small filling stones
falling apart like meat off a bone.

Home for a wildlife rock garden once more.
Ferns, stonecrop and cranesbill
gaining a foot hold
in the tilth and compost
from creeping mosses, ivy and lichens.
A hiding place for small rodents
sheltering among leaf-filled footings.
Wheatear eggs in the cavities.

Wind Turbine

Gosh, that's a big one!
Right next to the road.
Maybe that's why it looks huge,
relative to everything else.
It wobbles a bit when it's in full pelt.
Not sure these structures can withstand
a lot of 'swagger',
especially those windmills out at sea.
Or maybe that's just catastrophising.
Actually I think they're quite sculptural,
but not saying I want one in my back garden.

Think wind energy is supposed to be renewable
or sustainable.
Or both.
What does that mean exactly?
Is the turbine itself renewable, or its energy source
the wind?
And is turbine manufacture sustainable?
And what's the impact on carbon burden?
Renewable, sustainable.
Sustainable, renewable.
Probably terms invented for the convenience of humanity
and our inconvenient truths.
And somewhere in the cycle,
there will be carbon.

Peregrine

Like no other, I cleave the big skies,
my wings, shaped like boomerangs,
carve the blue majestically,
as I hunt way up,
winging above the cliff
until prey shows itself far below;

and then the fall begins.
Head first
swifter than any other,
faster and faster,
plunging with a hissing stoop!
And I strike,
talons pinning my prey,
before taking the carrion to my nest,
a scrape of twigs on a tower.
Eager young throats strain against each other
for food.

The breeze ruffles my underbelly,
white feathers tipped with black
like a coat of ermine.
Yellow of eye, yellow of beak,
talons of egg-yolk yellow,
bright against the slate grey
of *Falco peregrinus*.

Sky-dancer I

I don't follow the leader; there is no leader.
I move with my team-mates
to make a tear-drop, a twister, I'm a shape-shifter!

We swirl and gyrate, I am a sky-dancer!
Sometimes we make a figure of eight.
I don't follow the leader; there is no leader.

Thousands of wingbeats, the sound is a murmur.
I change direction in an instant, I don't go straight.
We make a tear-drop, a twister, we are shape-shifters!

We invite others to join us, we look after each other.
Humming like a prop-plane, our cloud pulsates.
I don't follow the leader; there is no leader.

Nobody stays on the edge of the crowd, we circle round
and move deeper.
A great morphing flock, in thousands we vibrate.
We make a tear-drop, a twister, we are shape-shifters!

We drop to our roost when the sky goes darker,
thousands together, we don't migrate.
I don't follow the leader; there is no leader.
I make a tear-drop, a twister, I'm a shape-shifter!

Sky-dancer II

I don't follow the leader; there is no leader.
I shape-shift with my neighbours,
changing direction in an instant
to swarm into a teardrop, a torpedo, a twister.
Well anything really, we don't go straight.
I am a sky-dancer, I swirl and gyrate!

We look after each other,
nobody stays on the edge of the crowd,
we circle round with our team-mates,
moving deeper into the flock,
inviting others to join us
in our dense black sun.

Thousands of wingbeats from iridescent wings,
thousands of us flying together for warmth.
Safety in numbers against the yellow hawk eye,
like the shoals and herds, nature protects.

Humming like a prop-plane, our cloud pulsates,
dropping out of the sky against the violets of dusk,
to roost for the night as the winter's day closes.

Willow

I weep, I sigh,
I almost touch the other side.
Is this an ox-bow?
Or is it a flood?
I don't know.
Mud, mud, glorious mud.
I planted my seed
and here I thrive.

But I am confused.
Was I here first?
Or was the water here before me?
Those lakes in the fields nearby –
sure they're not meant to be there.
Though the gulls and waders
don't waste any time
flocking to a new home.

Anyway,
a few of us happily cling
to the water's edge,
our feet in the mud.
Fluttering our silvery leaves,
a whispering shade,
boughs stooping as if to drink.
Our home here we have made.

I weep, I sigh,
I almost touch the other side.
I planted my seed
and here I thrive.

Teasel

Behold the statuesque teasel,
whose parched Autumn seedhead
belies its Summer beauty!
– Tiny purple flowers burst forth
in rings around the prickly influorescence,
bracts of vivid emerald curving upwards,
like the tail feathers of the lyre bird!

But the teasel doth tease!
The thirsty wild teasel
traps rainwater
in cups of sessile leaves
and ensnares sap-seeking prey.

The teasel doth tease!
The prickly fuller's teasel
raises the nap on woollen cloth
'washen well with water
and with teasels scratched'
in the fuller's handle house.

The teasel doth tease!
Its seven-foot stands
crowding out
opportunistic neighbours
on their waste-ground dwelling.

Behold the statuesque teasel,
whose parched Autumn seedhead
belies its Summer beauty!

Some Wessex Poets

Samuel Taylor Coleridge (1772 – 1834)
William Wordsworth (1770 – 1850)

I discovered on my journey through the Wessex landscapes, that the Quantock Hills are blessed with some riches in poetry; as mentioned earlier in my chapter on the Quantocks, **Samuel Taylor Coleridge** and **William Wordsworth** lived close to one another at Nether Stowey. Though residing there for only a short period, roughly from 1796 to 1798, their friendship was to give rise to some of the most important work in the history of English literature, with their *Lyrical Ballads* heralding the English Romantic Movement in poetry. Much of their work at this time was inspired by their walks together in the Quantock Hills; they walked almost every day, and often long distances.

    At Nether Stowey, Coleridge lived in a cottage now owned by the National Trust; he had befriended a local wealthy benefactor named Thomas Poole, who acquired the cottage for the Coleridge family. Coleridge became a frequent visitor to Poole's house next door, sometimes studying in his book parlour and sometimes writing in the garden.

    During this period, Coleridge produced his much praised 'conversation poems', *Frost at Midnight* and *This Lime-Tree Bower my Prison.* (The latter features in my poem *Lines from nether Stowey.*) He wrote at least eight conversation poems, all detailing life experiences, which lead the poet to examine nature and the role of poetry. At this time, Coleridge also famously wrote *The Rime of the Ancient Mariner,* believed to have been inspired by nearby Watchet Harbour, and *Kubla Khan.*

    Coleridge's fluid and imaginative poetry was very different from the structured poetry of the earlier period in the 1700s known as the Age of Enlightenment. Sadly though, he suffered from crippling bouts of mental ill-health, as well as physical disease. He was treated with laudanum but suffered an increasingly debilitating addiction to the drug; this together with a turbulent personal life, meant he never regained the success of his time in Nether Stowey.

    I have chosen here to reproduce an excerpt from *Frost at Midnight* – a poem in which Coleridge reflects overall on childhood, and emphasizes the benefits of being raised in the countryside. The excerpt below also alludes to the living conditions at Coleridge Cottage. An important theme in the poem is the fluttering ash in the fireplace, which is said to remind the reader of the delicate nature of memory, and how the past is like a shadow, barely hanging on:

The frost performs its secret ministry,
Unhelped by any wind. The owlet's cry
Came loud – and hark, again! Loud as before.
The inmates of my cottage, all at rest,
Have left me to that solitude, which suits
Abstruser musings: save that at my side
My cradled infant slumbers peacefully.
'Tis calm indeed! So calm, that it disturbs
And vexes meditation with its strange
And extreme silentness. Sea, hill, and wood,
This populous village! Sea, and hill, and wood,
With all the numberless goings-on of life,
Inaudible as dreams! The thin blue flame
Lies on my low-burnt fire, and quivers not;
Only that film, which fluttered on the grate,
Still flutters there, the sole unquiet thing.
Methinks its motion in this hush of nature
Gives it dim sympathies with me who live,
Making it a companionable form,
Whose puny flaps and freaks the idling Spirit
By its own moods interprets, everywhere
Echo or mirror seeking of itself,
And makes a toy of Thought....

Thomas Poole was a friend of several writers in the English Romantic Movement, among them William Wordsworth, whom he claimed to be the greatest man he had ever known. Wordsworth was born in Cumbria, one of four siblings, and was particularly close to his sister Dorothy. As a young man, Wordsworth developed a love of nature, which is reflected in his poetry, and although he began writing at school, he was not published until 1793. In 1795, Wordsworth and Dorothy moved to Dorset, and subsequently to the

Quantock Hills, to be close to Coleridge; there they rented the house known as Alfoxton Park (also with the assistance of Thomas Poole) some three miles from Coleridge Cottage. The Wordsworth/Coleridge friendship proved to be a very creatively productive relationship. In 1799, after a visit to Germany with Coleridge, the Wordsworths settled back in the lake District, at Dove Cottage in Grasmere.

Wordsworth was Poet Laureate from 1843 until his death in 1850. He remains one of the most recognizable names in English poetry and was a key figure among the Romantic poets. His great semi-autobiographical poem, *The Prelude*, which he had worked on since 1798, was published after his death.

I have included excerpts from Wordsworth's delightful poem entitled *Anecdotes for Fathers,* which he wrote whilst at Alfoxton Park, and which was first published in the 1798 edition of the *Lyrical Ballads.* The poem assumes the point of view of a father who recalls taking a walk with his five-year-old son, Edward, at Liswyn farm. During the walk the man contemplates his two favourite locations, Liswyn farm and Kilve's shore, and presses his son to declare his favourite of the two! Kilve features in my poem *At Kilve.*

...My thoughts on former pleasures ran;
I thought of Kilve's delightful shore...

Kilve, thought I, was a favoured place,
And so is Liswyn farm.

"Now tell me, had you rather be,"
I said, and took him by the arm,
"On Kilve's smooth shore, by the green sea,
Or here at Liswyn farm?"

In careless mood he looked at me,
While I still held him by the arm,
And said, "At Kilve I'd rather be
Than here at Liswyn Farm."...

"For, here are woods, hills smooth and warm:
There surely must some reason be
Why you would change sweet Liswyn farm
For Kilve by the green sea."...

Then did the boy his tongue unlock,
And eased his mind with this reply:
"St Kilve there was no weather-cock;
And that's the reason why."

The Lyrical Ballads

The *Lyrical Ballads* are a collection of poems by William Wordsworth and Samuel Taylor Coleridge, first published in 1798 and generally considered to have marked the beginning of the English Romantic Movement in literature. The publication became and remains a landmark, changing the course of English literature and poetry.

Most of the poems in the 1798 edition were written by Wordsworth, with Coleridge contributing only four poems to the collection (although these constituted about one-third of the book in length), including *The Rime of the Ancient Mariner*. The 1800 edition is famous for the *Preface to the Lyrical Ballads,* something that has come to be known as the Manifesto of Romanticism.

The Romantic period was an artistic and intellectual movement that originated in Europe towards the end of the 18th century. The purpose of the movement was to advocate for the importance of subjectivity and imagination, and appreciation of nature in society and culture, in response to the Age of Enlightenment and the Industrial Revolution.

Edward Thomas (1878 – 1917)

Moving on from the Romantic period, another notable poet associated with the Quantocks is **Edward Thomas**. Thomas has been described as having a crucial place in the development of 20th-century poetry, introducing a modern sensibility; his poems are written in a colloquial style, and frequently feature the English countryside.

In 1915, he enlisted in the British Army to fight in the First World War and was killed in action during the battle of Arras in 1917, soon after he arrived in France. At the time of his death, his poems were largely unpublished, but over the past century, his work as come to be cherished for its rare sustained vision of the natural world, and as 'a mirror of England' (Walter de la Mare). Thomas is sometimes considered to be a war poet, although few of his poems deal directly with his war experiences.

Early in 1913 Edward Thomas cycled from London to the Quantocks, writing an account of his journey commissioned by a publisher and titled *The Pursuit of Spring*. On his journey from Clapham to Coleridge's old home in Somerset he observed the landscape, the wildlife and the country ways and described them in his account. Ostensibly he was looking for the first signs of Spring, and, in passing, to check if there really was no weather-cock on the church at Kilve! Thomas reworked his notes and recollections into his poetry and there is one poem in particular – *For These* – which is undoubtedly inspired by the Quantocks; the poem has a lovely rhythmical lilt, helped by some lines that have the familiar trio of three elements:

*An acre of land between the shore and the hills,
Upon a ledge that shows my kingdoms three,
The lovely visible earth and sky and sea
Where what the curlew needs not, the farmer tills:*

*A house that shall love me as I love it,
Well-hedged, and honoured by a few ash trees
That linnets, greenfinches, and goldfinches
Shall often visit and make love in and flit:*

*A garden I need never go beyond,
Broken but neat, whose sunflowers every one
Are fit to be the sign of the Rising Sun:
A spring, a brook's bend, or at least a pond:*

*For these I ask not, but, neither too late
Nor yet too early, for what men call content,
And also that something may be sent
To be contented with, I ask of Fate.*

Anne Ridler (1912 – 2001)

I must mention **Anne Ridler** in connection with the Quantocks; Ridler's first book of poetry was published in 1939 and she continued to write poetry until her death in 2001. She was also a librettist and wrote several plays and verse plays. She was an editor at Faber and Faber, a colleague of T. S. Eliot, and a friend of C. S. Lewis.
Ridler first visited Aisholt in the Quantocks in 1930, returning many times throughout her life. This extract from *Aisholt Revisited* vividly describes the Quantock Hills:

These moors in August drank the burning sky,
And stretched out still thirsty, scorched by gorse,
Though the combes ran cool on either side
With waving fronds and streams to the red loam
And Appeasing pasture.

She also spoke of Wordsworth and Coleridge walking on the hills:
The Landscape was the occasion and the vessel.
So let our times beside the speaking streams,
In the secret cottage, or in the maze of combes,
By their intensity exist forever.

The poet **Charles Williams (1886-1945)** wrote of Aisholt too, and **Walter de la Mare (1873 – 1956)** declared upon visiting him:

Happy thou art to lie in that still room
Under the thick-thatched eaves in Aisholt Combe
Where sings the nightingale, where blooms the broom.

William Lisle Bowles (1762 – 1850)

William Lisle Bowles was an English, priest, poet and critic. Like many poets of his generation, he was educated at Oxford. In 1789 he published *Fourteen Sonnets*, which were very well received, not only by the general public, but also by his contemporaries such as Coleridge and Wordsworth. Coleridge credited him, alongside Charlotte Smith, with bringing about a general revival of the sonnet form in their generation. *Summer Evening at Home* was written in Cranborne Chase:

Come, lovely Evening! with thy smile of peace
Visit my humble dwelling; welcomed in,
Not with loud shouts, and the thronged city's din,
But with such sounds as bid all tumult cease
Of the sick heart; the grasshopper's faint pipe
Beneath the blades of dewy grass unripe,
The bleat of the lone lamb, the carol rude
Heard indistinctly from the village green,
The bird's last twitter, from the hedge-row seen,
Where, just before, the scattered crumbs I strewed,
To pay him for his farewell song;- all these
Touch soothingly the troubled ear, and please
The stilly-stirring fancies. Though my hours
(For I have drooped beneath life's early showers)
Pass lonely oft, and oft my heart is sad,
Yet I can leave the world, and feel most glad
To meet thee, Evening, here; here my own hand
Has decked with trees and shrubs the slopes around,
And whilst the leaves by dying airs are fanned,
Sweet to my spirit comes the farewell sound,
That seems to say: Forget the transient tear
Thy pale youth shed--Repose and Peace are here.

Lisle Bowles also wrote of the *Avenue in Savernake Forest*, near Marlborough in Wiltshire; in the opening of the poem, Bowles creates the atmosphere of the Forest, talking of 'arching height of ancient shade… within the gloom…in solemn shade…their dark branches…'

How soothing sound the gentle airs that move
The innumerable leaves, high overhead,
When autumn first, from the long avenue,
That lifts its arching height of ancient shade,
Steals here and there a leaf!
    Within the gloom,
In partial sunshine white, some trunks appear,
Studding the glens of fern; in solemn shade
Some mingle their dark branches, but yet all,
All make a sad sweet music, as they move,
Not undelightful to a stranger's heart.
They seem to say, in accents audible,
Farewell to summer, and farewell the strains
Of many a lithe and feathered chorister,
That through the depth of these incumbent woods
Made the long summer gladsome.
    I have heard
To the deep-mingling sounds of organs clear,
(When slow the choral anthem rose beneath),
The glimmering minster, through its pillared aisles,
Echo;- but not more sweet the vaulted roof
Rang to those linked harmonies, than here
The high wood answers to the lightest breath
Of nature.
    Oh, may such sweet music steal,
Soothing the cares of venerable age,
From public toil retired: may it awake,
As, still and slow, the sun of life declines,
Remembrances, not mournful, but most sweet;

May it, as oft beneath the sylvan shade
Their honoured owner strays, come like the sound
Of distant seraph harps, yet speaking clear!
How poor is every sound of earthly things,
When heaven's own music waits the just and pure!

Alfred Williams (1877 – 1930)

Alfred Williams was born at South Marston near Swindon, where he lived almost all his life. The son of a carpenter, he grew up in poverty after his father abandoned his wife and eight children. At 15 he went to work at the Great Western Railway in Swindon, where he became a hammerman in the stamping shop. It was whilst he was working at GWR that he carved out a career as a writer, a vocation that was entirely self-taught. He produced six volumes of poetry and thirteen books. As with many gifted writers who failed to receive acclaim whilst they were alive, Williams' legacy as a writer and chronicler of a disappearing world continues to grow long after his death. The following is an extract from his poem entitled *About Wiltshire*, from which it is clear that Williams' writing was rooted in his beloved Wiltshire:

Have you followed richer valleys? have you rounded fairer hills?
    Have you walked in broader avenues, or higher colonnades?
Have you wandered in such pastures, by such pleasant lakes and rills,
    Through such forest and plantations, through such thickets and such glades?
Can you name another county, you who've journeyed done and ended
    All the corners of the kingdom, travelled north and east and west,
Where all true association is more fully mixed and blended,
    And earth wears a fairer jewel on her palpitating breast?...

Thomas Hardy (1840 – 1928)

For many, the Dorset countryside, and indeed Wessex, are synonymous with the work of **Thomas Hardy.** The poet and novelist lived most of his life in Dorset, in Higher Bockhampton, east of Dorchester, in the early years, and subsequently at Max Gate, in the second half of his life. He trained as an architect, and practised in London, but he appeared never to feel at home in the Capital, and after five years returned to Dorset, to Max Gate, the house that he designed himself. His initial success came with his novels, in 1880, and although he regarded himself primarily as a poet, his first collection was not published until 1898. Thereafter, he committed himself to poetry.

Although his poems were initially not as well received as his novels had been, Hardy is now recognized as one of the great poets of the 20th Century, and his verse had a profound influence on later writers, including Robert Frost, W.H. Auden, Dylan Thomas, Philip Larkin and Ezra Pound. W.H. Auden spoke thus:

"My first master was Thomas Hardy, and I think I was very lucky in my choice. He was a good poet, perhaps a great one, but not too good. Much as I loved him, even I could see his diction was often clumsy and forced and that a lot of his poems were plain bad. This gave me hope where a flawless poet might have made me despair."

Thomas Hardy wrote in a great variety of poetic forms, and though in some ways a very traditional poet, he was unconventional, and experimented with slightly ungainly rhythms and colloquial diction. His poetic works are notable for melding ordinary conversation with verse.

Hardy often stays remorselessly with dullness, as in one his most accomplished poems, *Neutral Tones*, and he is a chronicler of deception and disappointment in both love and life. But Hardy's work endlessly embodies the soaring creativity of the freedom-loving imagination; his tender sensitivity to the human voice is at the core of his imagination.

Hardy was influenced both in his novels and in his poetry by Romanticism, including the poetry of William Wordsworth. There is something of Wordsworth and Coleridge in *Wessex Heights,* a beautiful poem in which Hardy describes the peace and comfort he finds from the Wessex hills, in contrast to the turmoil he experiences in the lowlands. In the poem (below) he muses upon lost loves, and his own life and development. This poem makes my heart soar, as do many of Hardy's poetic works, including *The Darkling Thrush*.

Hardy achieved such fame that he was awarded the Order of Merit, and his ashes are buried in Westminster Abbey.

*There are some heights in Wessex, shaped as if by a kindly hand
For thinking, dreaming, dying on, and at crises when I stand,
Say, on Ingpen Beacon eastward, or Wylls-Neck westwardly,
I seem where I was before my birth, and after death may be.*

*In the lowlands I have no comrade, not even the lone man's friend –
Her who suffereth long and is kind; accepts what he is too weak to mend:
Down there they are dubious and askance; there nobody thinks as I,
But mind-chains do not clank where one's next neighbour is in the sky.*

*In the towns I am tracked by phantoms having weird detective ways –
Shadows of beings who fellowed with myself of earlier days:
They hang about at places, and they say harsh heavy things –
Men with a wintry sneer, and women with tart disparagings.*

*Down there I seem to be false to myself, my simple self that was,
And is not now, and I see him watching, wondering what crass cause
Can have merged him into such a strange continuator as this,
Who yet has something in common with himself, my chrysalis.*

*I cannot go to the great grey Plain; there's a figure against the moon,
Nobody sees it but I, and it makes my breast beat out of tune;
I cannot go to the tall-spired town, being barred by the forms now passed
For everybody but me,
in whose long vision they stand there fast.*

There's a ghost at Yell'ham Bottom chiding loud at the fall of the night,
There's a ghost in Froom-side vale, thin-lipped and vague, in a shroud of white,
There is one in the railway train whenever I do not want it near,
I see its profile against the pane, saying what I would not hear.

As for one rare fair woman, I am now but a thought of hers,
I enter her mind and another thought succeeds me that she prefers;
Yet my love for her in its fulness she herself even did not know;
Well time cures hearts of tenderness, and now I can let her go.

So I am found on Ingpen Beacon, or on Wylls-Neck to the west,
Or else on homely Bulbarrow, or little Pilsdon Crest,
Where men have never cared to haunt, nor women have walked with me,
And ghosts then keep their distance; and I know some liberty.

Charlotte Smith (1749 – 1806)

Charlotte Smith was a novelist and poet who began writing in order to support her family. Despite ten novels, four children's books and other works, she saw herself mainly as a poet, and expected to be remembered as such. She is credited with reviving the sonnet, especially as a form to express personal emotion. Smith was born in London, but was somewhat peripatetic throughout her life, and lived at different times on the south coast, including Weymouth.

Largely forgotten by the mid-19th century, she has since been seen as a major precursor of the Romantic Movement in English literature. She wrote some beautiful poetry of the countryside, perhaps of a more modern feel than might be expected from the poetry of her era. Her notable poems include *Beachy Head,* and the delightful sonnet, *Written at Weymouth in Winter:*

The chill waves whiten in the sharp North-east;
Cold, cold the night-blast comes, with sullen sound,
And black and gloomy, like my cheerless breast:
Frowns the dark pier and lonely sea-view round.
Yet a few months – and on the peopled strand
Pleasure shall all her varied forms display;
Nymphs lightly tread the bright reflecting sand,
And proud sails whiten all the summer bay:
Then, from these winds that whistle keen and bleak,
Music's delightful melodies shall float
O'er the blue waters; but 'tis mine to seek
Rather, some unfrequented shade, remote
From sights and sounds of gaiety – I mourn
All that gave me delight – Ah! never to return.

William Barnes (1801 – 1886)

Multitalented poet William Barnes was born in Rushay, Dorset. He worked as a clerk and a schoolmaster before studying at the University of Cambridge, and becoming an ordained minister in the Church of England. He was a strong supporter of the Dorset dialect. When he died in 1886, an obituary read, "There is no doubt that he is the best pastoral poet we possess, the most sincere, the most genuine, and that the dialect is but a very thin veil hiding from us some of the most delicate and finished verse written in our time."

He wrote over 800 poems, and much other work, including a comprehensive English Grammar, quoting from more than 70 different languages. A linguistic purist, Barnes strongly advocated against borrowing foreign words into English, and instead supported the use and proliferation of "strong old Anglo-Saxon speech".

Dorset dialect features in my second book of poetry (*The Jurassic Coast, A Poet's Journey*), in which I write about Thomas Hardy's imaginary Egdon Heath, a poem full of local dialect (there is a glossary at the end of that book!). In *Evenen in the Village*, **William Barnes** writes about Dorset village life in the old dialect:

Now the light o' the west is a-turn'd to gloom,
  An' the men be at hwome vrom ground;
An' the bells be a-zendén all down the Coombe
  From tower, their mwoansome sound.
    An' the wind is still,
    An' the house-dogs do bark,
An' the rooks be a-vled to the elems high an' dark,
  An' the water do roar at mill.

An' the flickerén light drough the window-peäne
  Vrom the candle's dull fleäme do shoot,
An' young Jemmy the smith is a-gone down leäne,
  A-playén his shrill-vaiced flute.
      An' the miller's man,
      Do zit down at his ease
On the seat that is under the cluster o' trees,
  Wi' his pipe an' his cider can.

Here is another poem from Barnes, set in the Dorset village of Pentridge, on the edge of Cranborne Chase:

PENTRIDGE! – oh! my heart's a-swellen
Vull wi' jay to hear ye tellen
  Any news o' thik wold pleace,
An' the boughy hedges round it,
An' the river that do bound it
  Wi' his dark but glisnen feace.
Vor there's noo land, on either hand,
To me lik' Pentridge by the river.

Be there any leaves to quiver
On our aspen by the river?
  Doo er sheade the water still,
Where the rushes be a-growen,
Where the sullen Stour 's a-flowen
  Droo the meads vrom mill to mill?
Vor if a tree wer' dear to me,
Oh! 't wer' thik aspen by the river.

There, in eegrass newly shooten,
I did run on even vooten,
  Happy, awver new-mown land;
Or did zing wi' zingen drushes
While I plaited, out o' rushes,

Little baskets vor my hand;
Bezide the clote that there did float,
Wi' yollor blossoms, on the river.

When the western zun 's a-vallen,
What shill vaice is now a-callen
  Hwome the deairy to the pails?
Who do dreve em on, a-flingen
Wide-bow'd horns, or slowly zwingen
  Right an' left their tufty tails?
As they do goo a-huddled droo
The geate a-leaden up vrom river.

Bleaded grass is now a-shooten
Where the vloor wer' oonce our vooten,
  While the hall wer' still in pleace,
Stwones be looser in the wallen;
Hollor trees be nearer vallen;
  Ev'ry thing ha' chang'd its feace.
But still the neame do bide the seame,—
'T is Pentridge,— Pentridge by the river.

Henry Alford (1810 – 1871)

Henry Alford was from a Somerset family, and besides editing the works of John Donne, he published several volumes of his own verse. As with many poets, he evidently had multiple talents and professions! He wrote the sonnet below in praise of the Mendip Hills:

How grand beneath the feet that company
Of steep grey roofs and clustering pinnacles
Of the massy fane, brooding in majesty
Above the town that spreads among the dells!
Hark! the deep clock unrolls its voice of power;
And sweetly mellowed sound of chiming bells
Calling to prayer from out the central tower
Over the thickly timbered hollow dwells.
Meet worship-place for such a glorious stretch
Of sunny prospect, for these mighty hills,
And that dark solemn Tor, and all that reach
Of bright-green meadows, laced with silver rills,
Bounded by ranges of pale blue, that rise
To where white strips of sea are traced upon the skies.

I wanted to include Coleridge's poem (1795) entitled *Brockley Coomb*, which is beautifully evocative of the joy of hills, and how they can be good for the soul! The Coomb was said to be a favourite spot for Coleridge, and the poet **Arthur Hugh Clough** (1819 – 1861), devoted assistant to Florence Nightingale, also wrote a poem of the same name. Brockley coomb cuts in to the hills forming a northern outlier of the Mendips, and has been described as being "of singular beauty, sunk between steep rocks, rising at some points to the height of 300 feet. It is adorned with many noble trees, and all the fissures and ledges of the cliffs are enriched with a great variety of mosses and other forms of vegetation".

With many a pause and oft reverted eye
I climb the Coomb's ascent: sweet songsters near
Warble in shade their wild-wood melody:
Far off the unvarying Cuckoo soothes my ear.
Up scour the startling stragglers of the flock
That on green plots o'er precipices browse:
From the deep fissures of the naked rock
The Yew-tree bursts! Beneath its dark green boughs
(Mid which the May-thorn blends its blossoms white)
Where broad smooth stones jut out in mossy seats,
I rest: and now have gained the topmost site.
Ah! what a luxury of landscape meets
My gaze! Proud towers, and Cots more dear to me,
Elm-shadowed Fields, and prospect-bounding Sea.
Deep sighs my lonely heart: I drop the tear:
Enchanting spot! O were my Sara here.

About the Author

Amanda Kirkland Hampson (nee Adams) was born in 1959 and lived in Leigh-on-sea, Essex before attending University College Swansea, and subsequently the University of Aston in Birmingham, to study environmental biology. After a career principally as an editor in science and medicine, spanning over three decades, Amanda retired in 2015. Her professional life included several years as an editor at *The Lancet* medical journal and work abroad in over 20 countries. In contrast to her working life, she is now delightfully engaged in various branches of the Arts, and is also a keen walker and tennis player. She has lived in Wiltshire with her husband Keith since 2013.
AKHampsonPoetry@gmail.com
Instagram: akhampsonpoetry

The Artist

Sheila Haley has lived in the Vale of Pewsey for over twenty years. After retiring from a long service in schools administration, she joined a local group "So you think you can't draw!" where she discovered her gift for painting and drawing. Sheila has found the Wiltshire countryside and her love of village life are strong inspirations for her art works, and her detailed illustrations beautifully accompany the poems in this book. Sheila enjoys a full life – she has been involved in various community projects and was a police chaplain. In addition to her love of art, she is a keen table tennis player. Sheila also enjoys spending time with her three children and grandchildren.

Other Titles by the Author

This book, **A Celebration of Wiltshire in Poetry**, has been inspired by the natural history, landscape and heritage of this beautiful county. Wiltshire has a distinctive and ancient natural landscape, which is perhaps overlooked by travellers who pass through it, in search of coastal destinations further west. From flowers and trees to birds and bees, and villages and towns to hills and downs, this collection of 40 illustrated poems will be a delightful read for those who know Wiltshire, and countryside lovers alike.

'…And a soundless indigo mantle
falls, pinned to the universe
by a thousand twinklings
light-years away.'

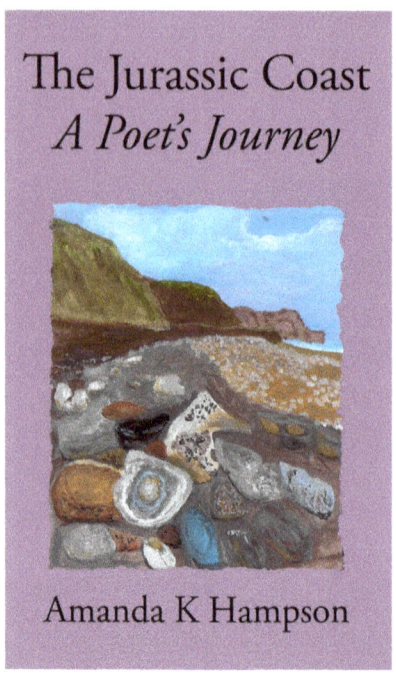

The Jurassic Coast, A Poet's Journey, is the author's second book of poetry, and as the title suggests, is a voyage in verse around the Dorset Coast in England. In 2001, the Jurassic Coast became England's first natural World Heritage Site, to be protected, conserved and passed intact to future generations. Its breathtaking beauty and wildness have been an inspiring source of riches for the varied poetry in this volume, together with the artist's vibrant illustrations.

'...Anning fossils,
entombed in a large grey pebbles,
are probed by tottering whimbrels
dodging tides of frothing circles.
Hear the screech of the hungry seagull
and the flap of the nesting kestrel,
across the reserve to a coastal idyll
where the Spit begins to dwindle.'

www.ingramcontent.com/pod-product-compliance
Lightning Source LLC
LaVergne TN
LVHW010308070426
835510LV00025B/3414